Helen Come Home

or Achilles the Heel

A Jazz Musical

Book and lyrics by
Jeremy James Taylor

Music by
David Nield

Samuel French — London
New York - Toronto - Hollywood

CHARACTERS

Zippy Zeus   Chief "Redcoat" at "Zeusland", Olympus-super-Mare's No. 1 Holiday Camp

Hera
Athene
Aphrodite }   Goddesses. Finalists in the Miss Olympus 3050 B.C. Beauty Competition

Helen   A Beauty Queen, and wife to Menelaus

King Agamemnon Leader of the Greek Army, brother to Menelaus

Odysseus
Achilles
Ajax
Menelaus }   Greek Generals

Sergeant-Major Soppycles   An officer in the Greek Army

Lance-Corporal O'Logarithm (Irish)

Private Epiglottis (the Camp Carpenter. Northern)
Private Pythagoras
Private Parthenon
Private Arthritis } Soppycles' Platoon

Chef Talia (the Camp Cook)

Greek Soldiers

Count Priam   King of Troy

Kid Paris
Duke Aeneas }   His sons

Cassandra   A Trojan Prophetess

Trojan Soldiers

PROLOGUE	The swimming-pool at Zeus Holiday Camp, Olympus-super-Mare. A cool summer evening
ACT I	The seashore outside Troy. A cool summer morning
ACT II	Inside the walls of Troy. Early the next morning

Time—3050 and 3040 B.C.

HELEN COME HOME or ACHILLES THE HEEL

A jazz-musical based on the story of The Trojan Horse.
First performed at Pangbourne College on Thursday,
23rd February, 1978. A slightly revised version was then
performed at Tiffin School and at The Young Vic
Theatre, London, in July 1978. The final version was
presented on The Fringe of The Edinburgh Festival,
1978, with the following cast of characters:

Zippy Zeus (your cheery compère)	Jonathan Hollins
Helen (Beauty Queen)	Ignacio Saiz
Kid Paris (current Cabaret King)	Gregg Butler
Hera (the rich Goddess)	Richard Sarsfield-Hall
Athene (the competitive Goddess)	Christopher Andrew
Aphrodite (the beautiful Goddess)	Richard Graves
General Odysseus (the sane)	Toby Nutt
General Menelaus (Helen's husband; an upright man)	James Burstall
King Agamemnon (a silly old buffer)	Kevin Price
General Achilles (the Heel)	James Goodsir
General Ajax (Achilles' sidekick)	Graham Kinsman
Sergeant-Major Soppycles	Alexander Hilton
Private Epiglottis (a thinker)	Ian Harrison
Lance Corporal O'Logarithm (a Celt)	Hilton Earl
Chef Talia (the Camp Cook)	Sean O Shea
Private Pythagoras (a Square-Basher)	David Tink
Private Arthritis (out of step)	Anthony Meineck
Private Parthenon (a pillar of strength)	Nicolas Andrews
Duke Aeneas (a Trojan Prince)	Hamish Darlington
Cassandra (some prophetess—with a message)	Dominic Straiton
Count Priam (King of Troy)	Mark Guthrie-Harrison
Greek Soldiers	Paul Cheesbrough, Angus Elliott, Mark Ridley, Richard Gaunt
Trojan Soldiers	Benedict Straiton, Pierre Chapat, Colin Campbell, Philip Jones, James Macpherson

Musical Director Ralph Allwood
Director Jeremy James Taylor

MUSICAL NUMBERS

ACT I

1	Variety Time	Zippy Zeus
3	The Bribe Song	Hera, Athene, Aphrodite, Helen, Kid Paris, Zippy Zeus
4	Variety Time (*reprise*)	Zippy Zeus
5	Ten Long Years	Chorus of Greeks
7	It's All A Load of Gor Blimey	Soppycles' Army
9	Daddy Agamemnon	Achilles and Agamemnon
11	It's All A Load of Gor Blimey (*reprise*)	Soppycles' Army
12	The Carpenter's Song	Odysseus with Epiglottis, O'Logarithm and Greek Chorus
13	The Odysseus Knock	Odysseus and Greek Chorus

ACT II

14	Roll It In	Trojan Army, Aeneas and Cassandra
15	Cassandra's Blues	Cassandra
16	Gotta Horse	Priam, Paris, Aeneas and Trojan Chorus
17	Greek Lullaby	Greek Chorus
18	Helen of Troy	Menelaus, Helen and semi-chorus
20	Finale	Tutti

The Music for this play is available from Samuel French Ltd. The missing Musical Numbers from the sequence above refer to Incidental Music Cues and are marked in the margins of the play-text

THE MUSIC

The accompaniment for musical numbers 1 to 4 is for organ bass and drums, though if necessary a piano may be used.

For the remainder of the piece the accompaniment is scored for four reeds (Alto Saxophone/Clarinet; Alto Saxophone/Clarinet; Tenor Saxophone/Clarinet/Bass Clarinet; Tenor Saxophone/Clarinet/Flute), three trumpets, two trombones, piano bass and drums, though if necessary it can be performed by piano bass and drums alone.

It is advisable to "mike" the soloists and indeed if the full band is used it is essential.

The score for numbers 1 to 4 contains a keyboard part which can be played without adaptation on the organ. The remainder of the score provides a keyboard part which players with a knowledge of jazz piano style will wish to use as a basis for interpretation. A good deal of the band material is written into this keyboard part which the pianist will omit when the full band is used.

D.N.

PRODUCTION NOTES

The Settings. These can be as simple or as complex as time, money and materials allow. There is a very short time between the end of the Prologue and the beginning of Act I—fifty seconds, to be precise, so the change from the swimming-pool to the Trojan seashore has to be carefully thought out. The original production made extensive use of different arrangements of rostra and steps with different fascias; Greek mosaic for the swimming-pool, yellow sand-stone boulders for the sea-wall, and large red stone-work for the walls inside Troy. The different levels provided by the rostra were particularly useful for the choreographed routines. The only piece of scenery that must be impressive and spectacular is The Horse which has to be built, by the Greek Army, on stage. (Note that, at the beginning of Act II, the Trojans have just *finished* hauling the horse into the city, so it doesn't actually *have* to move.) It will be very effective if there is a trap-door in the belly of the horse from which the Generals actually do emerge. In the original production, the horse consisted of a very strongly built basic framework, which included the trap-door and four thin wooden legs. This square-built structure was then "fleshed out" by cladding the sides and the legs with moulded bits of horse.

The Costumes. Obviously these are the decision of the Director and Designer involved. However, there are certain ideas which might prove useful. The Greek Army were kitted-out in a version of the Greek Chiton (the pleated skirt which is still worn by the Greek Army today), with simple white shirts, white tights and white shoes, berets and various additions like cummerbunds, hat-tassels and knee-garters. The Trojans were in the full Black-and-White Minstrel gear—stripey waistcoats, black trousers and shoes, spotted bow-ties, curly wigs, etc. The soloists were modern and varied in concept. Agamemnon and Priam were military; Achilles and Ajax, East End Gangster types; Kid Paris was hip American; Aeneas, a very stylish and different Black-and-White Minstrel type; Cassandra, a red-hot momma, earrings and all. Odysseus was in stripey blazer and boater and Menelaus in full boy-scout gear. Soppycles was in basic Greek Army gear but with a peaked cap and a cloak, while his platoon were also in regulation dress, though of all shapes and sizes. Epiglottis had a cloth cap and a carpenter's apron, Chef Talia wore a tall chef's hat, and O'Logarithm's trimmings were all Emerald Green! The Goddesses were as described in the text and as dazzling as possible and Helen in the Prologue was in stunning evening dress and very casually dressed—as if for the beach—in Act II. Zippy Zeus was rigged out with the worst possible taste in true "Pop D.J. style".

Properties. The only props that presented any problems were the seagull with the removable spear and Achilles' shoe with the spear embedded in it. These had to be specially made. Achilles' plaster cast was achieved by using a wellington boot and wrapping it in white bandage.

The Lighting. A follow-spot may be found useful, particularly during the songs, otherwise there are no special requirements.

A NOTE ABOUT CASTING

HELEN COME HOME was originally written for a cast of 11–13 year old boys. Thus, particularly with the "female" roles, a certain amount of doubling can take place. The three Goddesses in the Prologue were also able to play the parts of Trojans in Act II, as was Zippy Zeus (though he had to be smuggled off the stage after the de-sacking of The Trojans in order to get his black make-up off in time to return as Zippy Zeus at the end). By the same token, Priam, Aeneas and Cassandra could be used in the Greek chorus for Act I, though this means depleting the numbers of Greeks for Act II as well as some fairly hectic blacking up in the interval. The "audience" of holiday-makers watching the beauty competition in the Prologue can be made up of Trojan Chorus members and—if really pushed—members of Soppycles' Platoon.

J.J.T.

ACT I

PROLOGUE

Beside the swimming-pool at Zeusland, a very seedy Holiday Camp at Olympus-super-Mare. A cool summer evening in 3050 B.C.

There are some tables with umbrellas at which are seated assorted holiday-makers. A Waiter is serving drinks. As the organ bursts into music, Zippy Zeus, the garishly dressed compère, bounds cheerfully up to the microphone

SONG 1. *IT'S VARIETY TIME HERE IN ZEUSLAND*

Zippy Zeus (*singing*)

> It's variety time here in Zeusland,
> Golden Gooseland for us all,
> When it's cuppa-tea time here in Zeusland,
> Orange-juice land; have a ball . . .

He talks over the next six bars

> Good evening, ladies and gentlemen, boys and girls. It's wonderful to see your happy smiling faces here again enjoying the wonderful holiday spirit of Zeusland. Welcome again to variety time.

(*Singing*)

> There's no time for the whines or the whimpers
> At Olympus-super-Mare.
> But then should anyone do so, just give 'em some Ouzo,
> Come on, roll up and see the real fun of the fair.

Scattered applause. He continues, using the microphone

(*Speaking*) Thank you. Thank you. Thank you very much indeed, ladies and gentlemen, and welcome to Zeusland, the happy "fun-for-all-the-family" land here at Olympus-super-Mare where, tonight, we have the finals of the Golden Goddess of the Year Award for the title of Miss Olympus, three thousand and fifty B.C.

Fanfare   Cue 1a (1)

> Later on in the evening, we'll be having the Glamorous Granny divisional heats and the Knobbly Knee regional final for the dads, but first of all, fellahs, sit back and brace yourselves for the loveliest ladies this side of the Hellespont. Now, we'll be meeting our three ravishers in just a moment, but first, ladies and gents, you must meet two very special guests we've brought here to be with us tonight. First of all, all

the way from Sparta, the lovely winner of last year's Golden Goddess
Award who is here with her lucky husband, Menelaus, to pass on her
Miss Olympus sash to this year's lucky winner. Let's have a big hand
for the very beautiful—HELEN!

Cue 1a (2) *Fanfare*

> *Helen, dazzling in evening dress, etc., comes confidently on to the stage,
> with Menelaus trotting dutifully at her feet*

She blows kisses to everyone, a little to Menelaus' annoyance

Hi there, Helen, doll!
Helen Hi, Zippy. (*She blows Zippy Zeus a kiss*)

Menelaus tows Helen to their table at the side

Zippy Zeus And secondly, all the way from his home town, Troy, where
he's been doing Cabaret at the Coliseum Club, the judge of tonight's
big competition—and what a lucky guy he is—put your hands together
for the wonderful and talented KID PARIS!

Cue 1a (3) *Fanfare*

> *Kid Paris, all teeth, smiles and smarm, a kind of cheap version of Sammy
> Davis Junior, bounds on to the stage*

*All the adoring ladies by the poolside scream and swoon with disbelief and
excitement*

Kid Paris Good evening. Thank you. Thank you.
Zippy Zeus Hi there, Kid. Great to see you again.
Kid Paris Zippy, it's wonderful to be here again, man.

Hysterical laughter

Zippy Zeus Glad you could make it.
Kid Paris Try keepin' *me* away from a beauty competition!
Zippy Zeus (*howling with disproportionate laughter*) Nice one, Kid.
Reckon you and Helen'll make a great team tonight.
Kid Paris Helen?
Zippy Zeus Oh, Helen, baby, c'mon out here and meet the great Kid
Paris.

Helen moves slowly into the spotlight and offers her hand to Kid Paris

Helen (*into the microphone, very sexily*) Great to meet you, Kid.
Kid Paris (*totally disarmed, in love at first sight*) Wow!
Zippy Zeus (*unaware of this*) Now, make yourself comfortable, Kid.

*Paris, as if hypnotized, follows Helen back to her table. She introduces
Menelaus. He sits down, in a dream*

(*Prattling on*) Now, before we bring them on, let's tell you all about the
three gorgeous goddesses you've got to handle tonight. All the way from
Crete, we'll be meeting and greeting a neat chick, the bright-eyed

Athene with the dark brown hair! Number two is a real cutie from Carthage, the delectable Hera; and last, but certainly not least, a real stunner from Athens, the laughter-loving Aphrodite. How do you like that, Kid?

Kid Paris (*still ogling Helen*) Sounds just great, Zippy.

Zippy Zeus Okay. Well, just fasten your seat belts, 'cos here we go! The Competition comes in two parts. First, the girls will walk down in their evening gowns, and then comes our Zeusland speciality, the Miss Olympus Bribe Competition, when the girls get a chance to bribe lucky old Kid Paris there, with anything or any*one* they like! The best bribe wins. Should be fun! Are you ready, Kid?

Kid Paris Sure thing, man. I'm ready when Helen is.

Helen (*haughtily*) Any time you like, K.P.

Menelaus glowers

Zippy Zeus Okay. So here we go. Music, Maestro, please.

Walk-down music—instrumental   Cue 2

Hera, Athene and Aphrodite enter, and during the following move across to Kid Paris, then back c

Zippy Zeus, reading from a clipboard, describes their dresses as they move

First, ladies and gents, the lovely Hera. Hera is wearing an evening dress in yellow satin brocade cut to cling to the body and flare out. Oh, what a beautiful mover, she looks lovely and sweeps the streets clean as she goes. She's carrying a genuine mink stole—I don't know where she stole the mink from, but it sure looks nice! On her head is a diamante half-tiara with diamonds and pearls. She sewed the jewels on herself, then took them off because she decided they'd look better on the tiara! Her favourite hobbies are collecting rich husbands and knitting. Thank you very much, darling. Come on, let's hear it for Hera.

He leads the applause. Hera moves to her pedestal

Next we have the divine Athene. She's in a blue muslin print gown, with bandeau. The cigarette-holder is by courtesy of Double-Mew D. and H. Omega Wills. Athene is a very tough competitor. She won last year's Miss Athens Competition, beating Ariadne in the final over eleven rounds with two submissions and a knockout over a pinfall and a running flush. That seductive hair-do, by the way, won a gold medal at Crufts. Her hobbies include petit-point and wrestling in mud, and in the rest of her spare time she plays the flute and breeds ferrets. A big hand for your very own Athene!

Applause. Athene goes to her pedestal

And last, but most certainly not least, the winner of last year's Miss Water-Baby Competition, Aphrodite—she'd look flighty in a nightie! Aphrodite is quite a rover, in fact, that's a three-and-a-half litre bust you're looking at there, Kid! She's wearing a turquoise silk gown with her bust swathed in chiffon—sounds ticklish! She carries a white feather boa, though it doesn't seem to constrict her! Aphrodite was looking less well dressed than this when I last saw her—on page three of *The Helios*! Her favourite pastimes are deep-sea diving and growing melons. Thank you, Aphrodite.

The music finishes as Aphrodite swans off to join the others

Thank you, girls. Well, how about that then, Kid?
Kid Paris (*still preoccupied*) What?
Zippy Zeus Weren't they great?
Kid Paris (*looking straight down Helen's cleavage*) They sure are!
Menelaus (*getting to his feet in a fury*) That's absolutely disgusting. I'm not staying here to see my wife insulted by a foreigner. I'll see *you* later, Helen.

Menelaus stumps off past Zippy Zeus

Zippy Zeus is speechless

Kid Paris (*coming to the rescue*) Oh, yeah. Fantastic, Zeus baby. Sure is gonna be a tricky decision. What's next?
Zippy Zeus The highlight of the evening. The Miss Olympus Bribe Competition.

Cue 2a *Fanfare*

Come on, girls. And you, Kid. Take your places. Take it from the top, Maestro. Do your worst, girls, and may the best man win.

SONG 3.   *THE BRIBE SONG*

During the song the Girls mime or use props for their bribes

Hera	Hera will give you all the wealth of Midas, the King.
Athene	Athene will give you lands as wide as the sea.
Aphrodite	But Aphrodite will give the lovely Helen, the Queen,
All	Because it's vital that the title goes to me.
Hera	Riches and money
Athene **Aphrodite**	} The bitch is so funny.
Athene	Glory and honour.
Aphrodite **Hera**	} She doesn't begin.
Aphrodite	Helen as lover.
Athene **Hera**	} She'd sell you her mother.
All	You've got to believe me. I *just must* win.
Hera	Hera will give you all the wealth of Midas, the King.
Athene	Athene will give you lands as wide as the sea.
Aphrodite	But Aphrodite will give the lovely Helen, the Queen,
All	Because it's vital that the title goes to me.

Kid Paris	Three, four, five, six.
Aphrodite	Helen's the lady that'll dazzle your eyes
	Helen's the lady bringing luck to you
Kid Paris	Helen's the bribe that wins us both first prize
Tutti	You know, it's criminal what women'll devise
	Helen's a girl to make you sore
Hera	Helen's a girl to make you run
Athene	Helen ain't comin' home no more
Helen	(*as Kid Paris puts the sash on Aphrodite*)
Zippy Zeus	Hope you enjoy the prize you won tonight
	I'm thinkin', "Helen of Troy"
All Three	That sounds a real nice name
Tutti	We're drinking health to the winners, hope they feel all right.
	So Aphrodite has won. Everything's done.
	Now that the fun's over . . .

As the song fades, Zeus starts the hysterical applause

Menelaus returns, unseen by Zeus

Aphrodite weeps tears of helpless delight

Zippy Zeus Well, congratulations, Aphrodite. A swell bribe that richly deserves the title of Miss Olympus, three thousand and fifty B.C.

Fanfare

How about a couple of words? (*He thrusts the microphone at Aphrodite*)
Aphrodite (*coyly*) Well, thank you, Zippy, I sure am . . .
Zippy Zeus (*removing the microphone*) And what a lucky boy Kid Paris is!

Kid Paris claims Helen as his "bribe"

Menelaus (*aghast*) What?
Zippy Zeus (*seeing Menelaus*) Aah! And what bad luck on Menelaus. Still, that's the rules of the game here in Zeusland. You can't win them all.
Menelaus (*outraged*) But you can't just give away my wife like that!
Aphrodite Sure I can.
Zippy Zeus Sure she can! Haven't you read the brochure? You come to Zeusland, you play the game.
Kid Paris Sure thing, man.
Helen 'Bye 'bye, Menny.
Menelaus Now look here . . .
Zippy Zeus Say good-bye to the lady.
Menelaus You won't get away with this, Kid Paris. I'll be revenged on you, even if it takes ten years.

Menelaus storms off

Zippy Zeus (*watching Menelaus as he goes*) What a swell guy! Still, let's forget about him and wish the lucky pair here good luck on their journey back to Troy—and no hanky-panky on the boat, kids. That sea air can get you very excited!

Kid Paris Ciao, man.

Helen 'Bye, Zippy. (*She blows him, and everyone else, a kiss*)

Helen and Kid Paris swan off, hand in hand

Zippy Zeus So let's have a big hand for Helen and Paris and "Bon Voyage".

SONG 4. IT'S VARIETY TIME (reprise)

The CURTAINS *close behind Zippy Zeus as he speaks on over the first eight bars*

So that's all for tonight, folks. Hope you all enjoyed the show. See you later for the Glamorous Granny and Knobbly Knee Competitions. Meanwhile, it's 'Bye 'Bye Time . . .

(*Singing*)

Though it's time for the campers to leave now,
Don't you grieve now, there's no cause.
Remember, after the laughter has diminished we have finished off the
    show now,
So you can go now.
Make for the doors and let's hear your applause.

Zippy Zeus rushes off, waving a lot

Applause. The band play on into Song 4

The seashore outside Troy. Early morning, 3060 B.C.

The entire Athenian army is standing disconsolately about, singing

SONG 5. TEN LONG YEARS

Ten long years of sitting here by the water.
Ten long years outside the Trojan walls.
Ten years, fighting here for Zeus' fav'rite daughter.
Waiting til the city falls.
The Black-prowed ships are getting tired of their moorings.
They long to ride upon the bright salt seas.
The western winds from distant Athens are roaring.
Time to pack up and go back home to Greece.

Solo Have some sympathy for poor Menelaus,
A Spartan nobleman insulted by Troy.

Tutti The gods were deaf to our pleas and our prayers,
But woe today may tomorrow be joy.
Ain't got no time for the rose-fingered dawn,
Because tomorrow you may find us gone.

As the song ends, Odysseus and Menelaus come on, busily

Odysseus Come on, Fall in. Fall in. Enough of this mooning around. The sun's out, the seagulls are singing and King Agamemnon's on his way to give you his tenth anniversary speech, so get on parade.

Greek 1 Ten years of the same old speech.

Greek 2 And still nothing to show for it.

Menelaus Nothing to show for it? We may not have won back my wife yet but it's been ten good years of discipline and comradeship.

Greek 3 (*sarcastically*) Oh, jolly good show!

Greek 2 That's not what Achilles says.

Menelaus Achilles! Don't take any notice of that common cad. He's nothing but . . .

Odysseus Menelaus! Remember what I told you. Not in front of the children.

Menelaus Ah. Of course. Sorry, old chap. Slip of the old tongue.

Odysseus Have a jelly baby. (*He offers him a sweet from a large bag*)

Menelaus Gosh, thanks! (*He takes one*)

Agamemnon enters

Agamemnon (*as he arrives*) Ah. Odysseus, there you are. Where are the confounded men?

Odysseus Squad. Shun. *The squad leaps to attention*

Agamemnon spins round and sees them

Agamemnon Oh! Morning chaps. Lovely day. Perfect weather for fighting. Noses up. Chins to the grindstone and all that. (*A pregnant silence*) Yes Well . . . what are we here for?

Odysseus (*quietly*) Your speech, sir.

Agamemnon Oh, yes. Of course. That old thing. Now. Is everyone here? Where are Ajax and Achilles?

Odysseus They're—not present, sir.

Agamemnon Well, that's probably for the better. Let's leave it like that, shall we?

Menelaus But they *ought* to be here. Show a good front, and all that.

Odysseus I shouldn't bother. They know about this assembly, and they're not coming.

Menelaus Oh, golly.

Odysseus You know Achilles' feelings about this war, and whatever he thinks, Ajax agrees with.

Menelaus Little creep!

Odysseus Until something positive is done about winning back Helen, neither Achilles nor Ajax will take any further part in the war. They've washed their hands of the whole affair.

Agamemnon Jolly hygienic of them, but let's change the subject. I'll give *my* speech now, I think. (*He takes up his "speech-making" position, and peers shortsightedly at his notes*) Now then. (*He clears his throat*) It gives me great pleasure to declare this bridge open . . .

Menelaus (*staunchly*) Hear, hear.

Agamemnon (*grinding to a halt*) Bridge? That can't be right.

Odysseus quietly changes his notes for him

Ah! Sorry about that. Just testing!
Greek 1 Take two.
Menelaus Oh, lay off.
Agamemnon Now then, as you all know, nine years ago to this very day . . .

Odysseus whispers to him

As you all know, ten years ago to this very day, my beautiful sister-in-law, Helen, was cruelly and unlawfully stolen from her rightful husband, Menelaus here, and has been held over there in Troy ever since by that old idiot, Priam, and his upstart sons, Paris and Aeneas. Now, I've heard that some of you chaps aren't too happy with our progress. Now, nine er—ten years is a long time, I admit. Time for sons at home to grow into young men—daughters to grow into young women, and young pretty wives to grow into old ba . . . old pretty wives. But here, fighting by the walls of Troy, we have not been defeated. The gods have surely ordained that we should be rewarded for our patience.

Mumbles of approval start to spread

The Trojans must know that, when we meet in battle, we Greeks will be ready!

More approval

If they attack by sea, we'll be ready.

Ajax, carrying a violin-case, appears, walking backwards and looking up into the sky

Agamemnon does not notice Ajax

If they attack by land, we'll be ready. If they attack in daylight or in darkness, we will be . . .
Athenian Army (*now quite worked up*) READY!
Ajax (*simultaneously, shouting*) READY—AIM—

There is the squawk of a seagull overhead

FIRE!

The squawking suddenly becomes a screech. A speared seagull crashes down at Agamemnon's feet

Achilles slowly wanders on

Ajax picks the bird up

Good shot, boss. Nearly a gull's-eye.
Achilles Not bad. (*He extracts the spear*) But not good enough. A Greek should never miss, eh, Agamemnon?

Agamemnon shrugs

Least of all the great Achilles. Must be growing rusty. (*He tosses the carcass to Menelaus*) Here, Menelaus, a present for you. Have it stuffed. (*He sees the assembly*) What's this? Morning prayers?

Agamemnon No, Achilles. I'm addressing the men. It's our tenth anniversary here. Kindly respect that.

Achilles Anniversary! We should be mourning, not celebrating.

Ajax Quite!

Odysseus (*aside to Achilles*) This is no celebration, Achilles. It's a morale-boosting session. So just give him a chance, eh? Have a jelly-baby.

Achilles (*ignoring Odysseus' generous offer*) Blab. Blab. Blab. A lot of good that'll do to win the war.

Ajax Quite!

Menelaus Achilles, that's not very nice.

Achilles Wars aren't very nice, Menelaus, and this one's no exception.

Ajax Quite!

Agememnon (*impatiently*) Oh, someone shut him up.

Ajax (*keenly*) I'll do it. (*He opens his violin-case*)

Odysseus No, Ajax. Violence will get us nowhere.

Achilles Quite. (*He thumps Ajax*)

Odysseus Agamemnon, dismiss the men. Clearly this assembly is a waste of time.

Athenian Army Quite!

Agamemnon Oh, all right.

Odysseus Squad. Squad, left turn. Fall out.

The Army fall out and exit

Agamemnon That's it, chaps. Fall about. This always happens when I give one of my speeches. I never get a word in edgeways.

Odysseus (*as they go*) Never mind, sir. Have a jelly-baby.

Odysseus and Agamemnon exit

Menelaus (*finding himself alone, confronting Achilles and Ajax*) Now, let's keep this civil, Achilles. All this shouting and nastiness won't get us anywhere.

Achilles It might get us on that boat back to Athens instead of sitting around here getting old and damp. The men would be with *me* there, believe me.

Menelaus A mutiny? Ridiculous. They're a fine body of patriotic men.

Achilles Get knotted. They couldn't limp into battle, let alone march!

Menelaus Oh, come on, Achilles—(*going*)—just a quick chat.

Achilles Chat. Chat. Chat. Ten years of chat and look where it's got us.

Menelaus and Achilles exit

Ajax (*left alone, to the world at large*) I don't wanna chat. I wanna punch-up.

Ajax goes. The Platoon stagger into view

Music—Soppycles' Army Introduction   **Cue 6**

The Platoon shamble on

Seargeant-Major Squad, halt!

They screech to a halt and fall over one another. Sergeant-Major Soppycles regards them dubiously

Gor blimey. After ten years of training, I still reckon the only person who could drill you lot properly is a dentist! Come on. Organize your dress, get in line and pay attention.

They do—eventually

Now then, answer your name loud and clear if you're here. Keep quiet and shurrup if you're not. Are you wiv me, Private Pythagoras?

Pythagoras Well, I'm here, Sarge, if that's what you mean.

Sergeant-Major Gor blimey. Whassamarrer with you, Pythagoras? Can't you understand plain Greek? I can see you're here, can't I? Unless you're but a filament of my imagination.

Epiglottis You mean figment, Sarge.

Sergeant-Major Whassat? Private Epiglottis, you uttered?

Epiglottis Not filament, Sarge. Figment.

Sergeant-Major Oright. Oright, cleverclogs; just shut your booby trap, and listen. (*He consults his clipboard*) Now then. Private Pythagoras, present. Private Epiglottis, present. Chef Talia?

Each man as he answers takes a step forward, then back

Chef Here, Sarge.

Sergeant-Major Full marks. Private Parthenon?

Parthenon What, Sarge?

Sergeant-Major Are you present, or aren't you?

Parthenon (*stepping forward*) Yes, Sarge. (*He steps back*)

Sergeant-Major Ten out of ten. Private Arthritis. You wiv us?

Arthritis I think so, Sarge.

Sergeant-Major Well, keep tryin'. Last, but not least, Lance-Corporal O'Logarithm?

O'Logarithm (*who has a pleasant Irish accent*) Top of the morning, Sarge.

Sergeant-Major "Top of the mornin' ". None of your foreign lingo here, laddie. Why can't you say "Good mornin' ", like everybody else?

O'Logarithm "Good mornin' like everybody else," Sarge.

Sergeant-Major What's good about it? Gor blimey, flippin' weather! It's cold enough to make any Greek freeze! So. We're all 'ere, in a manner of speakin'. Now listen. Some of you brighter ones may have noticed that we've been sitting 'ere, outside Troy, for the past ten years and we don't seem to be makin' much progress. Ten years to this day it was when I first led you lot into action.

Pythagoras Congratulations, Sarge.

Sergeant-Major Thanks very much. (*He gives a double take*) Watch your step, Pythagoras, or it'll be square-bashin' for you, my lad. Gor blimey, no wonder we can't win the war with a load of stupid, illegitimate dumdums fightin' it, what can't even read and write proper.

Epiglottis "Illiterate", Sarge.

Sergeant-Major Whassat?

Epiglottis "Illiterate". That's the word for someone who can't read and write, not illegitimate.

Sergeant-Major Private Epiglottis. (*With a single finger he summons Epiglottis*)

Epiglottis humbly obeys

I may not be no classical scholar but I don't want no common soldier casting aspirations on my etymology. And as for the illegitimacy of Private Pythagoras, I 'ave no doubt that 'e's plain stupid. 'E's probably illiterate as well for all I know, but I don't think we should be conducting a public enquiry into the details of 'is parentage, so kindly get back in line and shut up.

Epiglottis returns to his place

Any questions? No? Good! Next.

O'Logarithm Sergeant.

Sergeant-Major Lance-Corporal O'Logarithm, you wished to spout?

O'Logarithm Yes, Sarge.

Sergeant-Major Well, out with it, and keep it clean.

O'Logarithm You just mentioned that we weren't making much progress with the war, Sarge!

Sergeant-Major My very words. 'Ere, you're quick for a foreigner. Where is it you come from?

O'Logarithm Crete, Sarge. (*Glassy-eyed*) The Emerald Isle.

Sergeant-Major Well, you can't 'elp that, but you're certainly showin' up all these Athenian dumdums.

O'Logarithm (*proudly*) I think we ought to think up our *own* plan.

Sergeant-Major You 'ear that, lads? We must think up our own plan.

Pythagoras Us?

Parthenon All by ourselves?

Arthritis Well, I'll help you.

Sergeant-Major Good lad, Arthritis. A "joint" effort, eh?

O'Logarithm If we could win back Helen without troubling Agamemnon, he'd appreciate it, I'm sure.

Chef General Agamemnon needs all the help he can get. Like an old-age pension!

Sergeant-Major Watch your lip, Chef Talia. That's very near to treason. Better cooks than you 'ave been boiled in their own cookin' pots for less—but I quite agree wiv you. (*To the rest*) Lance-Corporal O'Logarithm's words, gents, is the kind of thinkin' I want to see. 'Ave a gold star, O'Logarithm. It's music to the ears, son. Sheer flippin' music.

SONG 7. *IT'S ALL A LOAD OF GOR BLIMEY*

Platoon (*singing*)
It's all a load of Gor Blimey in Soppycles' Army
It's left, right, left, right, squad shun—(**Sergeant-Major** shurrup).

You know there's no-one denies us the big booby prize
'Cos when we lose, our excuses are second to none.

We'd take a good deal of beating at rapid retreating.
We only need the nod.
And we'll get it, I'll wager, from our own sergeant-major
Who's a great big stupid . . . (**Sergeant-Major** Squad, shun).

We know we're nothing more than a freak show,
But even though he knows all the platoon are thick
Soppy would sooner stick up for his lunatic gang.
Sergeant-Major (*speaking*) Squad, shun! Right turn! Sa-lute!
Platoon (*singing*)
It's all a load of Gor Blimey in Soppycles' Army
But though he can be hard to please,
For him we'd march at the double from all kinds of trouble
Till we're falling to crawling upon our knees.

We love him. We hate him. We can't underrate him
And the whole platoon agrees
That you couldn't demand a completer commander
Than Sergeant Soppycles.
Sergeant-Major Squad, salute!

*They salute. If the audience applauds, the Sergeant-Major tells them to
"Shurrup"*

Right, now. Let us not forget O'Logarithm's sage words. Here you are—
the cream of Greece's task force; acute, astute, prudent and perspi-
cacious, fleet of foot, nimble of wit and intelligent . . .
Pythagoras What does "intelligent" mean, Sarge?
Sergeant-Major Er . . . Tell 'im, O'Logarithm.
O'Logarithm Well, er . . .
Sergeant-Major Later! Meanwhile, rack your brains and stretch your
imaginations. The winnin' plan goes into operation tonight. No holds
barred.
Arthritis You mean we can fight dirty?
Chef Well, Achilles does.
Epiglottis Aye. But with the generals in their present mood, it wouldn't be
worth trying anything illicit.
Sergeant-Major If you don't watch your language, laddie, I'll 'ave your
tongue out!
Epiglottis No, Sarge. If you're "illicit" . . .
Sergeant-Major 'Ow dare you call me that! One more word . . .
Epiglottis (*giving up*) Sorry, Sarge.
Sergeant-Major Flippin' cheek! Now then, where were we? Ah yes—
tactics. If you 'ave a bright idea, take an aspirin, then come and tell me
all about it. We'll put it to the vote, and then I'll decide which one we
use. Now, my Mickey Mouse sundial says lunchtime. Move!

They line up

What's cookin' today, Chef Talia?

Chef Stiffato bladderwrackia, moussaka and mash with ice cream Lyons-maidia to follow.

The lads groan

Sergeant-Major Well, makes a change from Trojan horsemeat, eh?

There is a sudden burst of discussion off

Achilles (*off*) Agamemnon, if you think I'm waiting round here for another ten years till that old cow comes home, then you're thinking wrong!

Ajax (*off*) Quite.

Sergeant-Major Aha. Exit, stage right. Squaad. Squaad, shun, righ' turn. By the left. Quick. March.

March music   Cue 8

The Platoon shambles off

Sergeant-Major (*watching them go*) Lef', righ', lef', righ' . . .

Agamemnon appears, followed by Achilles and Ajax

(*Yelling*) Keep in step, Arthritis, you cripple. What do you think this is —"Come flippin' Dancing"?

The Sergeant-Major marches after the men

Agamemnon (*calling after him*) Fine work, Sergeant-Major, an example to us all. (*To Achilles*) Now that's the kind of spirit that'll outwit the Trojans.

Achilles Oh, plug the mug, Grandpa. Look, I came here to fight the Trojans, win back Helen and go home, not to sit around here, decomposing into a superannuated old relic. Right, Ajax?

Ajax Quite. What?

Agamemnon All right. But there's no need to jolly well shout all the time. They can probably hear you over in Troy. Before we know it, we'll have a revolt on our hands and, Zeus knows, the men are revolting enough already.

Achilles Oh, I get it. The famous Greek Democracy reigns only as long as it suits you, eh? You know very well, Agamemnon, that the best thing for you to do is to abandon this game and get back to Athens before you die here—of old age. Get into your famous boat and go home.

Agememnon That's absurd. Anyway, I don't think my poor old boat would get out of the bay, it's so old.

Ajax But it's supposed to be the finest warship in the fleet.

Agamemnon Ha! It was. "The launch that faced a thousand ships!" No more, I'm afraid. But, for all that, I'm not going to surrender. It'd be against the rules to give in now.

Achilles Oh waive the flippin' rules. Can't you recognize defeat when you see it?

Ajax Defeat? (*He looks at his feet*)

Agamemnon Let's have no talk of defeat, Achilles. Patience will bring its own rewards. Just wait and see.

SONG 9. *DADDY AGAMEMNON*

Achilles (*recitative*)
> Daddy, we've been waiting for far too long,
> This procrastination has been all wrong,
> 'Cos all this delaying has tempers fraying.
> We must stop playing.
> It matters less than you think it does.
> You're just a yes-man, that's bad because
> It's all got boring; you've been ignoring
> The basic issue, that's why I wish you'd
> Listen to me—
> 1. Daddy Agamemnon, sing another song.
> Daddy Agamemnon, we've been here too long.
> Daddy, we've been waiting and hesitating
> And hating every minute of doubt.
> Let's return to Athens and admit you're wrong,
> Let's return to Athens where we all belong.
> Drop your crazy theory, we're weary
> And bleary-eyed from scheming schemes and dreaming dreams that
> we'll win.
> Because from alpha to omega you know I've said
> That we should simply go home again and stay in bed.
> So get your hat and coat and board that boat
> And lose your dreary blues by cruising home instead.

Agamemnon
> 2. Don't be absurd, we must win back that bird
> Or the way to Hades will simply be made easy.
> Abandon that child, Daddy Zeus will go wild.
> While she's living in sin, don't give in. The Gods'll make a dreadful
> din.
> Don't complain. Use your brain.
> Find a ploy to enter Troy.
> Don't start quotin' at me, and take a note,
> Beware, take care of everything I've said.

Menelaus and Odysseus enter towards the end of the song. Menelaus is in the process of unwrapping one of Odysseus' toffees. They overhear the end of the argument

Menelaus Oh, I do wish all this squabbling would finish. It only makes everyone waxy. (*He drops his toffee paper*)

Ajax (*pointing at the paper*) Uh, uh! Keep Greece tidy!

Menelaus (*picking up the paper gingerly*) Gosh, sorry.

Odysseus Menelaus is right. Someone ought to do something constructive.

Achilles Sorry. I left my Lego at home.

Odysseus Oh cut the cackle, Achilles.

Ajax You can borrow my Meccano if you like.

The others ignore him

Achilles It's simply time someone saw sense around here. Quite apart from this futile war, the food is dreadful, the men are miserable, the boats are rotting and everyone's fed up with the whole thing. Not to mention the weather . . .

Ajax The weather?

Achilles (*snapping*) I told you not to mention that.

Ajax (*confused*) But you said . . .

Achille Oh, scrub it, Ajax.

Ajax Eh?

Odysseus Now relax, Ajax. Have a toffee.

Achilles Got any gob-stoppers?

Agamemnon Achilles, I won't have you talking to one of my bravest generals like that.

Achilles (*by now in a fury*) Ajax—one of your bravest generals? He isn't even fit to be a cleaner.

Menelaus Anyone who has fought as he has to save one of Greece's greatest ladies, certainly deserves more credit than anyone who defames her, like you do, Achilles.

Agamemnon Quite!

Achilles Helen! One of Greece's greatest ladies? That old polythene bag?

Menelaus (*stung*) I'm not staying here to be insulted by you, Achilles, you heel. That's just not cricket.

Menelaus stumps off

Agamemnon Well said, sir.

Odysseus Achilles, you're being very unfair. Think of all those barbarians in Troy. It's hell in there for Helen.

Ajax (*puzzled by the rhyme*) Hell in there for Helen?

Achilles Yeah. Hades for the ladies!

Odysseus And you mustn't bully her husband. He's a very sensitive chap. Menelaus has many layers, you know.

Ajax Many layers?

Achilles Ajax, old chap, why don't you just run off and oil your spear!

Ajax, somewhat bewildered by this last instruction gets his mini-spear out of his violin case and examines it, presumably for places to oil it

Agamemnon Oh, leave off, will you?

Achilles (*smugly*) That, my dear Agamemnon, is precisely what I'm about to do. I'm off, leaving by the very next boat. If you need me, I'll be packing in my tent. (*Sarcastically*) Happy hunting, Ajax!

Achilles sweeps out

Ajax (*knowingly*) You can't oil a spear!

A seagull squawks. Ajax's attention is caught by the sound. Like a cat stalking its prey, he stiffens and watches its progress across the sky, spear poised

Agamemnon (*aside to Odysseus*) You know, he may be brave, but I *think* he may be a bit stupid as well.

Odysseus You could just be right, sir.

Sergeant-Major (*roaring, off*) Pick your feet up, Pythagoras, you weak-kneed Greek freak!

Odysseus (*referring to the Sergeant-Major*) But there's always one stupider!

Ajax, about to let rip with his spear, gives out a great roar as the seagull lets rip first—right in his eye. He claps his hand to his face with a howl

(*Comforting him*) Well, at least he's a better shot than you are! Do you want a tissue?

Ajax (*as they go off, bitterly*) What do I want a tissue for? The flippin' bird's miles away by now!

Agamemnon, Ajax and Achilles go off

Cue 10 *Music—Soppycles' Army March*

The Platoon limp on in total disarray. Pythagoras is in a particular mess. They all end up facing in different directions

Sergeant-Major Squad—halt! Gor blimey. I dunno who picked you bunch of pansies, but 'e certainly didn't 'ave marchin' in mind when 'e did. Load of flippin' ballet dancers. Talk about the Greek camp!

Parthenon Perhaps that's why they give us these stupid costumes to wear, Sarge.

Laughter

Sergeant-Major Oright, oright, Aristophanes. When we need a comedy script, we'll let you know, so cut the funny quips. Chef Talia!

Chef Sarge?

Sergeant-Major Some fairly fruity complaints 'ave come to my notice from the ranks about today's lunch. There was a distinct flavour of seaweed about that moussaka and mash, and there was a great deal of bubblin' and squeakin' going on in the ranks. Seaweed! Do I detect right?

Chef It's just possible, Sarge. How did you guess?

Sergeant-Major (*holding his nose*) Alimentary, my dear Chef Talia. Let's 'ave no more of it, anyway. What's for supper—Trojan in the basket?

Chef (*poetically*) Domatosoupa de maison. Taramousalata à la Sparta butties or Psaria Sliced.

Sergeant-Major What, in Egon Ronay, is Psaria Sliced?

Chef Fish fingers, Sarge.

Pythagoras I didn't know fish had fingers.

Sergeant-Major (*readily*) Perhaps Private Pythagoras ought to go and tell 'is jokes to the Trojans, that way we'd be rid of 'em both. The enemy, stunned senseless wiv' boredom, an' Pythagoras 'ere doin' a passable imitation of Shish Kebab.

Pythagoras What's Shish Kebab?

Sergeant-Major (*tiredly*) Tell 'im, Chef Talia.

Chef Little bits of Greek meat skewered on a spear.

Pythagoras laughs, then realizes

Pythagoras Oh!

Sergeant-Major Oright. Enough jestin' and frivolity. What about O'Logarithm's little idea. Who's had any brainwaves?

Epiglottis (*shuffling forward*) Well, Sarge . . .

Sergeant-Major Oh Gawd! I might 'ave guessed. Why don't you stick to your woodwork, Epiglottis? Camp carpenters shouldn't 'ave brainwaves.

Epiglottis Well, this one does involve a bit of woodwork, Sarge.

Parthenon Oooh. Is it one of them war engines on wheels like the Romans use?

A cretin Romans?

Sergeant-Major Wait for it, soldier. Wait for it!

Epiglottis Well, Parthenon isn't far wrong. It *is* wooden and it *is* on wheels. The whole thing's a bit elaborate, but . . .

Sergeant-Major If you don't stop using them filthy words, laddie, I'll put you on a charge.

O'Logarithm Give him a chance, Sarge. This plan sounds quite interesting.

Sergeant-Major Come on, then, Epiglottis. Reveal all.

Epiglottis Well, in short, Sarge, it's a kind of monster, made of wood, on wheels, which is full of Greek soldiers which the Trojans will tow into their city.

Pythagoras A monster?

Epiglottis Yes. I've got the drawings here. It's a kind of horse. A Trojan Horse.

Sergeant-Major (*derisively*) How in flippin' heck do you make a Trojan Horse?

Pythagoras You steal his throat sweets!

General hilarity

Sergeant-Major Steal his throat sweets! (*He roars with laughter*) Nice one, Pythagoras. A Trojan Horse. Sounds ridiculous to me. There's a war on, you know, not a flippin' gymkhana! Now, what about the rest of you? I'm sure you're all brimmin' over with bright tactical ideas, aren't you?

Silence

Come on, come on. Now's your chance. Stand up straight, Arthritis, you're lookin' a bit limp. Now, for you, opportunity knocks.

More silence

Speak up, lad, I can't 'ear you.

Arthritis That could be because I didn't say anything, Sarge.
Sergeant-Major Good thinkin', lad. You'll go far. Pythagoras, what about you? A drachma for your thoughts.
Pythagoras I'm trying, Sarge.
Sergeant-Major Yeah. Very tryin'. Private Parthenon, got any constructive suggestions?
Parthenon I'd rather go home.
Sergeant-Major Gor blimey, whassamarrer wiv' you, Parthenon? You crumblin' or something? You used to be a pillar of strength. The original Ionic man. 'Ow about you, Chef Talia? Got any ideas cookin', or are you goin' to pot as well?
Chef Well, Sarge, I did have one thought.

The Platoon reel back, stunned

Sergeant-Major So tell us—slowly.
Chef Well, we've spent ten years trying to break through the gates or climb over the walls, but nobody has yet tried to get *under* them.
Sergeant-Major Under 'em? Don't be daft.
Chef We could dig a tunnel.
O'Logarithm A tunnel!
Arthritis Sounds dead boring to me.
Sergeant-Major Oright, Arthritis. No need to be inflammatory.
Pythagoras But they'd see us digging.
Chef Not if we did it at night!
Parthenon (*suddenly illuminated*) Then it would be dark!
Sergeant-Major (*as he gets the idea*) Eureka! Eu—flippin'—reka! A 'ole. Then up we all pops at dead of night inside the city—
Chef —capture Helen—
Arthritis —and bundle her back here—
Pythagoras —through the tunnel—
Parthenon —our tunnel—
Sergeant-Major —and *we've* won the war.

A great cheer from the lads

Chef Talia, get peelin' them fish fingers and then sharpen your ladle. We start diggin' tonight! Gor blimey. I dunno 'ow I think of them; really I don't. I shall be a general before you can say "Armichedes".
Epiglottis You mean "Archimedes", Sarge.
Sergeant-Major Oh, wrap up, Epiglottis. Go ride your wooden horse!

The lads roar with laughter

SONG 11. *IT'S ALL A LOAD OF GOR BLIMEY* (*reprise*)

Platoon (*singing*)
It's all a load of Gor Blimey in Soppycles' Army
But no-one here's prepared to bet
That Epiglottis, of course, will win the war on his horse,
He's such a great big, stupid . . .

Sergeant-Major Get fell in!

Platoon (*singing*)

But it's by digging our tunnel the war'll be won:
We'll all be weighed down with V.C.s.
Then they'll hail our commander the new Alexander,
That's Sergeant Soppycles

Sergeant-Major (*as the song ends*) Squad, shun. Right turn. Quick march!

The Sergeant-Major and Platoon, except for O'Logarithm and Epiglottis, march off

O'Logarithm and Epiglottis watch them go

Epiglottis (*fuming*) Eeee! That hard-boiled dimwit!

O'Logarithm What's that?

Epiglottis That half-baked banana!

O'Logarithm Who, Soppycles? He's not that bad.

Epiglottis He's daft as a brush. A tunnel! I ask you. Those poor dumb loonies'll be nowt but spear-fodder.

O'Logarithm Well, let's face it. Your wooden horse doesn't exactly sound like a winner!

Epiglottis He never even gave me a chance to explain, the gormless goop . . .

O'Logarithm Now, calm down. Whatever's got into you?

Epiglottis *I've* had a great idea and *he* won't listen. That's what.

O'Logarithm Well, I'll listen. Tell me, and we'll build it together.

Epiglottis No chance. We need the whole Athenian army to work this one.

Odysseus enters at the back, sees the two soldiers, and hides himself. He listens to their conversation

It's one for the big guns, this.

O'Logarithm Well, you never know. It might get to the ears of one of them.

Epiglottis Some hopes!

O'Logarithm (*sitting Epiglottis down*) So, it's a big wooden horse on wheels?

Epiglottis Aye, full of Greek soldiers.

O'Logarithm (*the joker*) What—the wheels?

Epiglottis Aye, that's right . . . No! The horse, you fool. Look, here's the plan. (*He gets out the large drawing*)

O'Logarithm (*impressed*) By Alexander!

Epiglottis We build it and leave it here on the shore where the Trojans can see it. Then, at night, we all sail round the corner in a hurry.

O'Logarithm I'd rather go in a boat. (*He roars with laughter at his own joke, then grinds to a halt under Epiglottis' steely stare*)

Epiglottis Will you shurrup!

O'Logarithm Sorry. Go on.

Epiglottis (*tentatively*) Well. Then we get a volunteer. That'll be you, a spy who is left behind, makes sure he is captured by the Trojans, and tells them that the Greeks have thrown in the towel and gone home.

O'Logarithm (*impressed*) Oh, I see.

Epiglottis Now, here's the key. The horse, you say, is a good luck offering to the great goddess Athene, to speed them on their way back to Greece. But if they were simply to tow the horse into Troy, the luck would be transferred to them and our fleet would meet with disaster at sea.

O'Logarithm Hmn. Clever. But why me?

Epiglottis Well, you Cretins have all the charming qualities needed to flatter old Priam.

O'Logarithm (*flattered*) Oh, thanks very much.

Epiglottis You're also a good liar.

O'Logarithm That's a lie. I don't . . .

Epiglottis (*gaining control*) I haven't finished yet.

O'Logarithm (*resigned*) What else?

Epiglottis Well, once they've towed it in, it's a right doddle. You simply wait for the Trojans to finish their Mardi Gras celebrations; then, while they're all snoring drunkenly, you open up the trapdoor in the horse . . .

O'Logarithm The pony trapdoor, you mean?

Epiglottis Pony trap . . .? Oh, pony trap. (*He laughs, then realizes*) Hey. Will you stop cracking stupid gags and let me finish.

O'Logarithm shrugs

You let them out of the horse—open the gates where the rest of the army are waiting—and Bob's your uncle. We just tie up a few drunken Trojans, the city's ours, and Helen's back with Menelaus. What do you think?

O'Logarithm Well, it sounds great. There is one problem, though. What if they don't bite at the lucky omen bit? Bit—horse—"bit"—d'you get it?

Epiglottis does get it, and is not impressed

Well, that could be nasty. All those Athenians sitting inside the horse's tummy—no food, no drink, B.O., and all that; and the Trojans might just come and burn it.

Odysseus comes forward and stands just behind them

Epiglottis Not if you do your job well enough. Old Priam's so dumb he'll believe anything.

Odysseus It would be worth having a standby plan, though.

Epiglottis I suppose you're right. But what . . . (*He realizes*) Odysseus! What the fllippin' heck are you doin' here?

They both leap to attention

Sir!

Odysseus I overheard your plan. Fascinating. Ingenious, if I may say so.

Epiglottis Aye, of course you can, sir.

Odysseus (*holding out a bag*) Have a pontefract cake.

Epiglottis Ooh. Ta! (*He takes one*).

Odysseus (*offering the bag to O'Logarithm*) But O'Logarithm's right. It needs just one more bit of bait to tempt the Trojans.

O'Logarithm What if it was built just too big to go through the city gates?

Epiglottis Too big? What good's that?

Odysseus Oh, I see. Priam would then be doubly keen to get it into the city.

O'Logarithm Right! So he has to knock down the gate to get it in.

Epiglottis But why in Hades should he?

O'Logarithm 'Cos I suggest it to him, see?

Epiglottis Oh! Clever.

Odysseus Brilliant. The psychological approach. You Cretins aren't as daft as you look. Here, let's see your drawing, Epiglottis.

Epiglottis hands him the drawing

Now, how do we build this thing, and what of?

Epiglottis Well, you plan your structure from the ears to the wheels. Select your timber, best is Phrygian deal. You get it measured; you're ready to saw, and then you build the biggest horse in the war. (*He slides into rhythm*) Take a hammer, a chisel, a brace and a bit, a back-screwed butterfly hinge, and a moulded architrave'll perfectly fit a fine-tooled saddle and fringe.

SONG 12. *THE CARPENTER'S SONG*

Odysseus Oh I see; you mean—(*He sings*)
    You plan your structure from the ears to the wheels.
    Select your timber, best is Phrygian deal.
    You get it measured, you're ready to saw.
    And now you build the biggest horse in the war.
    Take a hammer, chisel, and a brace and a bit,
    A back-screwed butterfly hinge,
    And a moulded architrave'll perfectly fit
    A fine-tooled saddle and fringe.

All Three   Oh, you plan your structure from the ears to the wheels.

During this verse the Greek army come in to listen. They do a tap routine during the instrumental break, using hammers, chisels, etc.,

    Select your timber, best is Phrygian deal.
    You get it measured, you're ready to saw.
    And now you build the biggest horse in the war.
    Take a hammer, chisel, and a brace and a bit,
    A back-screwed butterfly hinge,
    And a moulded architrave'll perfectly fit
    A fine-tooled saddle and fringe.

Odysseus   Now a hollow belly with a bridle-joint floor
    With a dovetailed halving, all planed.
    You check it's screwed and countersunk, with single-lock door
    And rat-tailed hemp for the mane.

Full Chorus Yeah!
Then the wheels, all mounted with an ovolo mould
On fine-greased bearings that'll easily roll.
We line the housing with platinum foil:
A varnish coat of Polynesian oil.
Then we fill the baby with Athenian brawn
And leave her here on the shore.
When the Trojans see it in the light of the dawn,
We'll soon be winning the war.

Instrumental break—soft shoe shuffle

Yeah!
Then the wheels, all mounted with an ovolo mould
On fine-greased bearings that'll easily roll.
We line the housing with platinum foil:
A varnish of Polynesian oil.
Then we fill the baby with Athenian brawn
And leave her here on the shore.
When the Trojans see it in the light of the dawn
We'll soon be winning the war.
When the Trojans see it in the light of the dawn
We'll soon be winning the war.

Odysseus Epiglottis, my friend, you've hit the nail right on the head.
O'Logarithm, nip off and fetch Agamemnon, will you?

O'Logarithm You bet, sir. My pleasure, sir.

O'Logarithm salutes and goes

Odysseus (*turning to the rest of the assembled company*) Gentlemen, thanks
to Epiglottis here, all our troubles could be at an end.

First Greek So what's the story, sir?

Odysseus A brilliant plan to trick the Trojans. Look, here's the design.
(*He holds it up*)

Second Greek (*looking at it*) Funny-looking dog.

Epiglottis No, you dimwit. It's an 'orse.

Third Greek Well, I don't know about the Trojans, but it sure beats me.

Agamemnon bustles on with O'Logarithm

Agamemnon Now, Odysseus, what the devil's all this about a cardboard
box?

Menelaus and Ajax follow Agamemnon on

Odysseus No, sir, a wooden horse. Look, here's Epiglottis' design.

Agamemnon (*peering at it*) Well I'm jiggered. Funny-looking dog.

Odysseus No, sir, it's a horse which we fill with Athenians, and trick the
Trojans into wheeling it into their city. Then—Bob's your uncle.

Agamemnon Well, it's all Greek to me, but it sounds super.

Epiglottis Thank you, sir.

Menelaus Golly, yes.

Epiglottis Thanks.
Ajax Yeah, great.
Epiglottis Ta.
Agamemnon So, it'll be the pipe and slippers in front of the fire with Helen now, eh, Menelaus?
Menelaus Pipe and slippers? When I see that woman, I'll tear her limb from limb. And as for Paris, when I've finished with that pigeon-toed foreigner he'll have knock-kneed armpits, he'll think with a squint and walk with a lisp. Just you wait!

During the above, Sergeant-Major Soppycles marches on carrying a bucket and spade. When he sees the assembled company he stops in his tracks and starts to tiptoe off

Agamemnon Golly! (*He spots Soppycles*) Sergeant-Major! Where are you off to in such a hurry? Doing some gardening?
Sergeant-Major (*thrown*) Er, no, your Honour. To another part of the field. I've got a bit of a problem with me privates. Thank you, sir.

The Sergeant-Major salutes frantically, catching himself in the face with his bucket, and exits fast

Agamemnon Curious fellow.
O'Logarithm Oh, I shouldn't worry about him, sir.
Epiglottis Just let him play with his bucket and spade.
Odysseus (*getting back to the point*) So we're all agreed, are we? What are we waiting for?

During the above, Achilles slinks on with his baggage in his hand

Achilles Your eleventh anniversary, I imagine. What's this? Another hen party?
Menelaus No, Achilles; actually it's a council of war.
Achilles Aha. Be prepared, eh? Well, keep plotting, gents. I'll see you back in Athens. C'mon, Ajax.
Ajax (*bravely*) 'Bye.
Achilles (*sneering*) You're staying?
Ajax I'm staying.
Agamemnon Good show.
Menelaus Hear, hear.
Achilles Well, bully for you, bonehead.
Odysseus You still leaving, then, Achilles?
Achilles Right now, Odysseus. (*He turns to go, then checks himself*) Oh, how's the target practice been going, Ajax?
Ajax Oh, not too bad. (*He produces his spear from its case. There is a fish impaled on it*) Fish kebab!
Achilles Well, since *I* won't be needing it any more, and *you* most certainly will, let me give you a parting gift. My battle spear. Tried and true. Double top every time.
Ajax Ooh! Ta, boss. (*He takes the spear proudly*)
Achilles But be careful with it. It's sharp. Happy hunting. I'll see you all

back in Athens. Even you, Agamemnon, if you're not pushing up the daisies by then. (*He pauses for effect, but there isn't much*) Toodle-oo.

Achilles goes, somewhat half-heartedly

Menelaus And good riddance to bad rubbish!
Odysseus Menelaus!
Menelaus Sorry.
Agamemnon Well, at least he left us his spear!

There is the squawk of a seagull. Ajax stiffens and spots it. So does everyone else. Slowly, pointing with their hands, they follow the bird's progress across the sky and off in the direction Achilles has just taken. The bird still squawking, Ajax takes aim and, with a huge cry, lets go with the spear. It hurtles off into the distance. As it finds its mark, there is an anguished yell. Everybody looks horrified

> *Slowly, Achilles drags himself back on stage. The spear is embedded in his left heel. He reaches the middle of the stage, regards Ajax for a moment, then lets rip*

Achilles Yooouu dim-witted, loopy, half-baked, gormless idiot!
Ajax (*simply*) I hit your foot.
Achilles You hit my foot.
Ajax Sorry, boss.
Menelaus Oh golly!
Agememnon Well, bang goes the journey home. Hard cheese, Achilles. Welcome back. Now, let's get building. Odysseus . . .!
Odysseus Right, Epiglottis. The floor is yours.
Epiglottis Oh no, sir. You do it. You've got the rhythm.
Odysseus Okay. So, who's gonna help me build this baby?
Ajax I reckon I should have a bash!
Odysseus You can say that again!
Ajax I reckon I should have a bash!

SONG 13. *ODYSSEUS KNOCK*

During the song, the following things happen: (1) The Greek Army, under the command of Epiglottis and O'Logarithm, build the wooden horse. (2) Ajax, amid the furious reprimands of Achilles, apologizes to him and wraps up Achilles' foot in an enormous plaster cast. The heel is particularly exaggerated. (3) The Sergeant-Major and the rest of his Platoon tiptoe across the stage, unseen by the rest of the army. They are armed with shovels and picks. Seeing the horse, they fall about with silent laughter as they go off

Odysseus (*singing*)

1. Take a saw, take a hammer, take a pile of wood.
   You scrape it and you shape it, till it's feelin' good.
   You build the biggest monster that you ever saw.
   Everybody build a mighty horse to win the Trojan war.
Chorus   Well, let's knock. Knock. Knock.
   For Menelaus, let's knock. Knock. Knock. Knock.

This rockin' horse'll really rock. Rock. Rock. Rock.
Let's hear the old Odysseus knock.

Odysseus 2. Screw a shoe, nail a tail and build a mane with a rein.
They'll wonder what we've left upon the Trojan plain.
Make a flank with a plank and build a hoof and a paw.
Not only—

Chorus One—
Odysseus Not only—
Chorus Two—
Odysseus Not only—
Chorus Three—
Odysseus But make it—
Chorus Four.
So let's knock. Knock. Knock.
For Menelaus, let's knock. Knock. Knock. Knock.
This rockin' horse'll really rock. Rock. Rock. Rock.
Let's hear the old Odysseus knock.

There is an instrumental break during which the horse is built

Odysseus Then we sail around the corner on the evenin' tide
Leavin' all the mighty heroes ridin', hidin' inside
And we'll simply tell the Trojans it's a lucky toy,
An' when we leave it, they'll believe it and they'll heave it into
Troy.
Chorus So let's knock. Knock. Knock.
For Menelaus, let's knock. Knock. Knock. Knock.
This rockin' horse'll really rock. Rock. Rock. Rock.
Let's hear the old Oddyseus knock.
Let's hear the old Odysseus knock.
Let's hear the old Odysseus knock.
Let's hear the old, the old Odysseus knock!

*The Greeks form a triumphant tableau around their horse, Achilles limps to
the front to have a look at it, Agamemnon shakes hands energetically with
Epiglottis; as—*

the CURTAIN *falls*

ACT II

Inside the walls of Troy. Dawn

In silhouette can be seen the outline of the great horse. The Trojans have just towed it into the city. As it grinds to a halt, the Trojans, wiping the sweat off their brows, coil up the ropes and gather around the "monster", looking at it in awe. Duke Aeneas is supervising the operation. The rest of the Trojans, all in bright, stripey waistcoats, are, like Duke Aeneas, Kid Paris and Count Priam, black. Cassandra, a big, black-momma of a prophetess, is regarding the monster with a certain amount of doubt

SONG 14. ROLL IT IN

The music starts before the CURTAIN *rises*

Solo Voice
(with others joining in gradually)

    Roll it in. Roll it in. Through the gates go roll it in.
    De Fates command the Trojans, roll it in.
    Them Greeks, they leave a token
    And the Gods above have spoken
    Dat de siege will soon be broken. Roll it in.

The CURTAIN *rises, to semi-darkness*

Full

    Roll it in. Roll it in. Through the gates go roll it in.
    De Fates command the Trojans, roll it in.
    Them Greeks, they leave a token
    And the Gods above have spoken
    Dat de siege will soon be broken. Roll it in.

    As them wheels begin to thunder
    There's few and plenty wonder,
    But our Massa's will be done to roll it in.
    There are those who say we're crazy.
    There are those who too damn lazy.
    But that Priam King, he says we roll it in.

The Lights snap up

Solo	King Priam gave the order, roll it in.
Chorus	Roll it in.
Solo	King Priam gave the order, roll it in.
Chorus	Roll it in.
Solo	King Priam gave the order not to leave it by the water.
	That Priam say we oughta roll it in.

Solo	Some say this thing mean sadness. Roll it in.
Chorus	Roll it in.
Solo	Some say this thing mean sadness. Roll it in.
Chorus	Roll it in.
Solo	Some say this thing mean sadness. Some say this thing mean gladness.
	But I say this mean madness. Roll it in.
Solo	That thing mean milk and honey. Roll it in.
Chorus	Roll it in.
Solo	That thing mean milk and honey. Roll it in.
Chorus	Roll it in.
Solo	That thing mean milk and honey. Lots of food and lots of money.
Another Solo	I think that real funny. Roll it in.
Chorus	Ha! Ha! Roll it in, etc.
Cassandra	It's some trick to buy back Helen. Roll it out.
Chorus	No it ain't.
Cassandra	It's some trick to buy back Helen. Roll it out.
Chorus	No it ain't.
Cassandra	It's some trick to buy back Helen. No-one listenin' what I'm tellin'.
	'Cos everybody's yellin' no it ain't.
Chorus	No it ain't.
	Roll it in, etc.

As them wheels begin to thunder
There's few and plenty wonder,
But our Massa's will be done to roll it in.
There are those who say we're crazy.
There are those who too damn lazy.
But that Priam King, he says we roll it in. Yeah!

First Trojan Well, I dunno what dis ting means, but I reckon it spells trouble. Whadda you think, Duke Aeneas?

Aeneas Well, Count Priam done said tow it in, so we have to tow it in, but I ain't so sure why.

Second Trojan Well, it sure is mighty fine, whatever it is. (*He spits*)

First Trojan Well, I still don't like it. How's about you, Cassandra?

Cassandra (*doomily*) I feel danger has entered our city! Danger an' doom! Dis monster no good! It spell danger an' woe!

Second Trojan Oh shut up, Cassandra, you miserable old goat. (*He spits*)

Aeneas Yeah. Soul sister. Everythin' you ever say is jus' danger an' woe. Some prophetess. Why not prophesy somet'in' nice for a change, eh?

Second Trojan Yeah. Like an end to dis war. Dat's what dis monster means. I knows it.

They all spit

Kid Paris, casually dressed, strolls on with Helen, even more casually dressed, on his arm

Kid Paris (*looking at the horse*) So, you got it in here, guys. How d'you manage dat?

Aeneas Dey's rebuildin' de main gate now. Ole Priam's supervisin' it hisself. I cain't tink why he's so keen.

Helen Ooh! K.P., what a big monster. What is it?

Kid Paris Now, don' you worry yo' priddy little head about it, Helen honey. Count Priam jus' thinks dis is some kinda monster. A message from the Gods, he say.

They sit at the Twelve Blues Bar. A Waiter serves them drinks

Cassandra It spells doom, I tell you. Danger and woe!

Helen Oh shuttup, Cassandra, you miserable old goat.

Kid Paris Now careful, sugar-pie. Don't talk to Auntie Cassandra like dat. It ain't nice.

Aeneas Dat's right.

Kid Paris Why, she was tellin' me only dis mornin', dat all the omens are bad. Right, Cassandra?

Cassandra Right, K.P. The cockerel started cluckin'.

Kid Paris Right.

Cassandra The temple flame went out.

Kid Paris Right.

SONG 15. *CASSANDRA'S BLUES*

The Blues should ideally be sung by Cassandra. However, depending on the singers available, it can be given to Aeneas or Kid Paris. A little re-allocation of the previous four speeches is then necessary

Cassandra (*speaking*) And the omens for the Trojans look bad . . .
   1. At the dawnin' just this mornin', the sun was turnin' blood red.
   At the dawnin' just this mornin', the sun was turnin' blood red.
You heard what I said.
   That dawnin's just one warnin'. If you start yawnin', you're dead.
   2. The sacred bulls have started mooin', it's necessary to go.
   The sacred bulls have started mooin', it's necessary to go.
I tell you it's so.
   That mooin' spells our ruin. That's me an' you in for woe.

Instrumental interlude. During it, she speaks

Them Gods are scowlin'. The owls have started howlin'. Them fowls need disembowellin'. They won't stop yowlin'. The holy hawks are squawkin'. They won't stop talkin'. Let's all get walkin'. Geeze, it's hot out here. Who's got a drink?

Someone goes over with a drink for Cassandra

Because the omens for the Trojans look bad.
   3. Come on, start your prayin'. This stranger's dang'rous, I know.
   Ev'ryone start your prayin'. This stranger's dang'rous, I know.
So get up and go.

'Cos while you're prayin', there'll be slayin', so I'm sayin' there'll be
Danger and woe.
That's all.
Second Trojan Look, if these omens mean trouble, where's it comin'
from? Dere ain't no troublemakers around. Dem lily-livered Greeks
have deserted us and all sailed back to Athens.

A cheer from the troops

Aeneas Dat's true.
Kid Paris You hear dat, honey?
Helen You mean no more trouble from silly old Menelaus any more?
Kid Paris Right on, honey-pie, no more Menelaus.
Helen Gee, that's great, K.P.
Kid Paris (*aside to Helen*) Honey, I wish you wouldn't keep callin'
me K.P.
Helen Why not? It's easier than Kid Paris.
Kid Paris Yeah. But it makes me sound like some kinda nut.
Helen Well, I like it. Can I have another drink?
Kid Paris Sure thing, doll. Waiter! A drink for the lady. Ouzo on the
rocks, and make it slippy.

The Waiter shoots out

Priam (*off, yelling*) I cain't see him now. I'ze busy. Scram!
Helen Who's that?
Aeneas Guess who!
Priam (*off*) Whaddya mean, it's urgent? I can only see people by ar-
rangement. Ain't you ever heard of "By Royal Appointment"?
Skedaddle.
Kid Paris It's big daddy!

Priam bursts in

Priam Geeze. Anybody'd think I got nothin' better to do than stand
around'n talk all day. Hi there, kids! Okay, so let's have a look at this
baby. My, ain't she a beauty? Real home cookin'. Whaddaya reckon
this monster is, then, Aeneas?
Aeneas Well, Pa, I dunno . . .
Priam It's a gift from dem Gods, I tell you. True Boogaloo. Right, K.P.?
Kid Paris Well, I ain't so sure, Pa.
Cassandra (*getting violent*) It spells woe; I say. Woe—woe—woe!
Priam Woah there, Cassandra, sister. Quit the gum beatin'. Someone get
her outa here, before the fire brigade comes.

Cassandra is led off, muttering

Dat's it, blackbird, make tracks. Now come on, Trojans. (*He looks at
them all*) Cheer up! Big Daddy Priam here's tellin' you there ain'ı
gonna be no woe. Them chicken-hearted Greeks have give up an' left
that seaside as empty as an Athenian skull. Kid Paris here can keep his
beautiful Helen after all. (*He waves to Helen*) Hi, there, cup-cake!

Helen Hi, Count Pri.

Priam You like my monster?

Helen Sure do, Count.

Priam Dere now, a lady of taste. (*He wanders over to the horse*) We done gone won the war, *and* got ourselves dis beautiful monster into the bargain. Wheyhey! (*He yanks the horse's tail energetically*)

The horse neighs. There are screams of terror. Everyone hides and cowers in fear

Priam Who was dat?

Silence

C'mon. C'mon. Speak up. I won't have no insolence in my city.

Kid Paris It was the monster, Pa.

Priam Button your lip, Satchelmouth.

Aeneas He's right, Pa.

Priam Whassat?

Aeneas He's right. It was the monster.

Kid Paris You done pulled the tail thing, an' the monster spoke.

Aeneas Pull it again.

Priam Sure thing. (*He pulls the tail*)

The horse neighs

Hey. Youz right. It talks, too. It *is* from heaven, I tell you. Listen here. (*He shouts up*) Hey you, monster man. Dem Greeks've gone home. Yeah? (*He pulls the tail*)

The horse neighs

See! And Kid Paris can keep his beautiful Helen after all, eh? (*He pulls the tail*)

The horse neighs

Wheyhey! We gotta winner here. I ain't no theologian, but I *knew* them Gods were Trojan!

A Guard rushes in suddenly

Guard Massa Priam, Massa Priam, we captured this white guy lurkin' around the walls.

Aeneas White guy?

Guard I reckon he's a Greek. You want for us to bring him in here?

Priam A white guy? Outa sight. Wheel him in. Let's see what he gotta say.

Guard Okay, boss. Stick around.

The Guard exits

Priam C'mon everyone. Skit. We gotta do some big talkin'. C'mon. Move it. Move it!

The Trojans move off, muttering excitedly

Kid Paris Now, don't you trust him, Pa. I reckon he's like this monster here. Dangerous.

Aeneas Dat's right. He's gonna tell us a whole buncha lies.

Priam Okay, guys. Cool it. Let's listen to dis rooster anyway. Could be good for a gas.

Kid Paris Pa, I'se not gonna listen. I reckon . . .

Priam (*sharply*) Wrap it, Kid. I'se the boss round here, and you's gonna listen. Okay?

Kid Paris (*resigned*) Okay, Pa.

The Guard piles in, shoving O'Logarithm in front of him

Guard Here's the coloured guy, boss.

O'Logarithm (*indignantly*) I'm not coloured. I'm white.

Aeneas No, man. You's the coloured one. You ain't black. (*He roars with laughter*)

Priam Hey, look at dis, guys. A real Greek freak.

They surround O'Logarithm and examine him

O'Logarithm I'm no Athenian. I'm from Crete. The Emerald Isle.

Kid Paris Dat could explain the funny accent.

O'Logarithm I'd sooner be from Troy than from Athens. So don't call me a Greek.

Kid Paris Okay, wise guy. You cain't kid me.

Priam No. You can't kid Kid Paris.

O'Logarithm Oh. So *you* are the great Kid Paris. The one who won Helen?

Kid Paris Dat's me.

Helen (*waving*) Hello, soldier.

O'Logarithm Top o' the mornin' to you. (*He does a quadruple take*) Wow!

Aeneas Kid Paris won Helen? Dat's rich. You Greeks are fightin' 'cos you say he stole Helen.

Priam Dat's right, man. He's s'pose to have stole her.

O'Logarithm But I'm trying to tell you I hate the Greeks. That's why I'm here. I want to get my revenge on them.

Priam Now, jus' a minute, sunshine lips. You crazy or somet'n? You's tryin' to tell us you wanna be here?

Aeneas You wanna be here?

Kid Paris You wanna be here?

O'Logarithm I wanna be here!

Priam
Aeneas } He *is* crazy! } (*Speaking together*)
Kid Paris

O'Logarithm (*to Priam*) Who are *you*, anyway?

Priam Me? I am Pri-am!

Kid Paris (*astonished*) You mean, you didn't know?

O'Logarithm No. I'm afraid you all look alike to me. I can't think why.

Aeneas We all wear the same coloured socks. That confuses a lotta people! (*He roars with laughter*)

Kid Paris So, whaddaya here for, kiddo? Why ain't you scuttlin' back to Athens with the rest of them coward Greeks?

O'Logarithm Oh, I let them go without me. They won't bother to come back and find me when they discover I'm missing.

Priam Why not, white guy?

O'Logarithm They'll be too worried about their precious good-luck charm.

Priam (*suspiciously*) Good-luck charm?

O'Logarithm Yes. I see you've already towed it in here. Very wise.

Priam Oh, you mean my monster?

O'Logarithm No. I mean Epiglottis's horse.

Kid Paris Epi-who's what?

O'Logarithm Epiglottis's horse. This thing.

Aeneas Oh. So that's what it is. A horse?

Priam (*astonished*) A horse.

O'Logarithm That's right.

Priam Now, you's takin' me for a ride!

O'Logarithm No, sir. It's a sacred horse, built to honour the Goddess Athene who will give the Greeks good luck on their journey home.

Priam Oh yeah?

O'Logarithm That's right. But I stayed behind to suggest to you to bring it into the city.

Priam But we done that, dumdum.

O'Logarithm I know. Even knocking down walls to get it in here. Very, very clever.

Kid Paris You mean that?

O'Logarithm Dat's right.

Priam (*flattered*) Hey. Home cookin' man! I told you we should knock down dem gates.

Aeneas And now the luck is ours?

O'Logarithm Correct.

Priam⎫
Aeneas ⎬ Home cookin'! ⎬ (*Speaking together*)
Kid Paris⎭

Priam (*delightedly*) Aeneas, call the men, quick. Step'n fetch 'em. We must celebrate. An' you must join us, white guy. Hey, what's yo' name?

O'Logarithm Lance-Corporal O'Logarithm.

Priam Somethin' else! Okay, white guy. Stick around.

The rest of the Trojans enter, hustled in by Aeneas and Kid Paris

Come on in, you guys. Come on. Now listen, you cats. I got somet'n to tell you. Our friend, O'Greeky here, has just proven me to be right about this here monster.

Priam starts to speak in rhythm, as does everyone else

He says that here we gotta lucky charm.

Tutti   A lucky charm?

Priam	Yeah! A lucky charm.
	Ain't you ever hearda the sport a kings?
Solo	The sport a kings?
Priam	Yeah! The sport a kings.
	This quadruped monster is a lucky horse.
Tutti	A lucky horse?
Solo	Oh, a lucky horse.
Priam	Ain't dat right, Greek boy?
O'Logarithm	
	Sure is, Maestro.
Priam	Wha' did I say?

Aeneas
Kid Paris } You said right. } (*Speaking together*)

Priam Well, c'mon kids, let's have a ball.
Tutti Yeah!
Priam Take it from the top, then, Maestro.

SONG 16. *GOTTA HORSE*

Priam	Gotta horse. No baloney. The neatest pony there ever could be.
	What a horse. I say it don't look phoney to me. See
	A lotta horse, some quadruped.
	No pony trap, like what you said.
	And this omen, boy, means your home in Troy will be free.
Kid Paris	So this nag ain't no gag.
Aeneas	So this mare ain't no snare.

Kid Paris
Aeneas } So this mule ain't foolin' us. Keep it cool and you'll see.

Tutti	We gotta horse a lucky charm
	Gotta horse to keep us all from harm.
	So let's celebrate this fated date. What a horse.
Full Chorus	What a horse. Lucky star. The Kentucky Derby is run today
	And of course, a lucky horseshoe goes a long way, say
	Let's swing and have a fling. Let's be alive. Let's jive and sing
	'Cos our jazz has razamatazz, and we gotta horse.
	Keep it loose. No excuse. Come on dance. Take your chance.
	Simply pass the bottle and who knows what'll ensue, you
	Gotta move, just do the conga and step around that bucking bronco
	And prance and dance and clap your hands for the horse.
	Yeah! Yeah! Yeah!

Instrumental interlude and dance. During the dance sequence, Waiters distribute drinks in brisk profusion. Helen and Kid Paris are particularly stylish on the dance floor. Priam drinks a great deal

Hit the booze. Just can't lose. Have a ball, you'll all feel ten feet tall.

Come on, rock and roll. This foal ain't singin' the blues,
oobi doobi doo wah bah da da
Who's gonna say we're not the tops? Just drink until the
last man drops.
Let the whole thing go, and just say hello to the horse.
(*Speaking*) Hello, horse!
Hit the floor. Sing Glory Hallelujah—well, just one more.
Hot a worse! Gosh. Guess I'm sloshed. What a horse!
Course. Thunk I'm drink.
What a day. Say. Hit the hay.

Priam   Does it kick? Say. Kiss me quick!

*By this time the entire Trojan Army has collapsed on the floor as a result of
the drink that has been circulating during the song. O'Logarithm is the only
one left on his feet. There is a great deal of snoring, etc.*

Cue 16a *Music. Greek descent from the horse*

*As soon as he is sure everything is safe, O'Logarithm goes to the foot of the
horse and whistles. A ladder appears. One by one the Generals and Epiglottis
come down. Ajax has to help Achilles with his plastered foot. Odysseus
instructs O'Logarithm to open the city gates. He does so—if necessary going
off stage*

*The rest of the Greeks tiptoe in. Each is armed with a sack. They distribute
themselves so that each Trojan is covered by a Greek*

SONG 17. *GREEK LULLABY*

All Greeks Sleep my pretty little Trojans in the moonlight's beams.
But beware. Take care. This omen is not what it seems.
Just you relax on the floor and have a good snore
Before we just shake you and awake you from your drunken
dreams.
You thought your horse couldn't lose
So took to the booze and had a good snooze.
You backed the fav'rite to win, but now you must sing the
blues.
Sleep my pretty little Trojans in the moonlight's beams.
But beware, take care, this omen is not what it seems.
Round your inebriate heap your enemies creep. Don't peep
Till we wake you—shake you—take you from your drunken ...
sleep.

*During the pauses in the last line, indicated by dashes, the Greeks tiptoe into
position prior to "sacking" the Trojans. During the instrumental drum
break, marked by three dots (. . .) the Trojans are unceremoniously awoken
and bundled into sacks by the Greeks*

Odysseus (*surveying the pile of sacks*) Great work, O'Logarithm.
Epiglottis Aye. Well done, mate. It worked like a dream.

Odysseus Now, which one of these is Count Priam?

O'Logarithm The one that makes the most noise, sir.

Aeneas (*from under his sack, very drunkenly, singing*) Roll it in. Roll it in . . . Through the gates go roll it in . . .

Trojans (*to a man*) HIC!

Odysseus How about that one?

O'Logarithm (*checking*) No. That's Duke Aeneas.

Ajax Hey, here's a big one. (*He struggles with the sack*) It's a bit tight.

Agamemnon They all seem a bit tight to me.

Cassandra Woe! Woe! I told you so!

Achilles Oh shut up, you miserable old goat.

Priam (*suddenly, with a hiccup, and a violent belch, singing in muttered strains*) Gotta horse. No baloney. The neatest pony there ever could be.

Trojans HIC!

O'Logarithm This sounds like him. The King of the Swingers.

Priam Hey! Who turned the light out? Where's the bar?

O'Logarithm Yes, sir. That's your baby.

Agamemnon Unwrap him!

Priam is unwrapped

What funny little men!

Priam (*exploding from his sack*) Gee, thanks, man. Now let's get this party movin' again. C'mon! Bring on the dancin' girls. Heat up the music. Blow, you Gabriels, blow. (*He grinds to a halt, turns and regards the Athenians*) Why, hello there!

Agamemnon Count Priam, I presume.

Priam Right on, wise guy. Do I know you?

Odysseus Meet King Agamemnon, leader of the Athenian Army.

Ajax The boss.

Epiglottis And now, King of Troy.

There is an enormous cheer from the Greek Army

Agamemnon How do you do. Jolly pleased to meet you. (*He extends his hand*)

Priam (*suddenly realizing*) Hey! Where did yous all crawl in here from?

O'Logarithm From inside your lucky horse.

Priam My lucky horse? Oh, I get it. The pony trap. So smooth-talker here—(*indicating O'Logarithm*)—was takin' us for a ride all along, eh?

Epiglottis You've got it.

Ajax And now we've got the whole war wrapped up.

Priam (*looking at his own army*) Well, I've heard of the sacking of Troy, but this is ridiculous. So. What happens next?

Odysseus Have a chocolate-drop.

Priam (*pointedly*) Never touch the stuff!

Achilles (*moving forward*) Try a licorice comfit, eh?

Priam Watch it! (*He sees Achilles' heel*) Hey! Dig that crazy footwear! That's a big chilblain. Wha's the trouble, big boy? White man's version of gangrene, eh?

Ajax laughs

Achilles Where's my spear, Ajax?

Priam Oh, hop it, peg-leg. (*To Agamemnon*) So, what are you gonna do to us now?

Agamemnon Well, that's rather up to Menelaus, isn't it?

Priam Menelaus?

Agamemnon (*in Priam's ear*) Yes. Er—Helen's "ex", you know.

Achilles Well, come on, Menelaus. Now's your big chance. Ten years is a long time to wait, but you said you'd tear her limb from limb, and now you can.

Menelaus (*rooted to the spot, and trembling*) Oh, golly!

Agamemnon Come on, Menelaus, old chap, meet Count Priam and tell him what you're going to do.

Menelaus (*looking at Priam*) Oh, golly!

Priam Okay, white guy, no need to get personal.

Achilles So tell him, man. You want Helen.

Menelaus (*with his eyes firmly shut*) I want Helen—

Achilles —brought before you—

Menelaus —brought before me—

Achilles —and you'll make her pay for her treachery—

Ajax —and tear her limb from limb . . .

Kid Paris (*from inside his sack*) No! Not my Helen! No!

Agamemnon What the devil's that?

Priam Dat's Paris.

O'Logarithm He's plastered.

Odysseus Half the cast is plastered.

O'Logarithm A plastered-cast!

Menelaus (*in frustration*) Oh, golly!

Kid Paris Let me outa here!

Odysseus Shall we let them out, sir?

Agamemnon Yes, debag the lot of them.

The Athenians de-sack the Trojans

At the same time, Helen slinks on

Achilles And someone find the lady.

Agamemnon Right. Where's Helen?

Helen She's right here, King Aggie.

The entire Athenian Army spin round and see her. Menelaus is the only one who does not look

Greek Army Wow!

Menelaus (*taking a deep breath, still not looking at her*) Helen, you unfaithful woman! How could you behave as shamelessly as you have? For ten years now, two great cities have been at war over your treachery and I have sworn that, when we won the war, I would give you the treatment you deserved, and believe me, I will, as soon as I get my hands on you . . .

At this moment Helen's hand comes to rest on Menelaus' shoulder. He turns, sees her, and crumbles

Oh, golly!

Helen (*seductively*) Hello, Menny.

Menelaus (*gulping*) Hello. (*He tries, half-heartedly, to go on*) Now don't do that, Helen, otherwise I won't be answerable for my actions.

Helen You never were, Menny dear, when you got excited.

Menelaus Gosh, lay off, Helen. Don't look at me like that.

Helen Why not?

Menelaus Oh, golly.

Kid Paris (*yelling*) Helen!

Helen (*spinning on Kid Paris, showing her true colours*) Wrap it. K.P. Your time's up. (*Instantly charming*) It's great to see you again, Menny. Ten years is a long time.

Menelaus Well, actually, it's *pretty* good to see you again.

SONG 18. *HELEN OF TROY*

(*Speaking over the Introduction*) I must say you're looking as super as ever.

Helen You reckon so?

Menelaus Oh golly, I think I feel a song coming on! (*He sings*)⟧
Helen of Troy. Oh boy. I'm overflowing with joy.
Seeing your face, this place is heaven.
Year after year, I thought I'd lost you for ever,ꞌ
So far, yet so near.
Now that you're here, my dear, it's heaven.
Though I had wished you were dead, instead,
I felt I'd melt at the turn of your head.
We've been fighting too long. I realize I've been wrong, so wrong,
And it's taken so long.
After the war, I'm sure, I'll love you ever more and more
But tell me it's true, it's you? That's heaven.

Helen Paris has used me so bad.

Menelaus He did?

Helen He's mad.

Menelaus No kid.

Helen I'm glad you did what you did.

Menelaus Nothing but a cad.

Helen Just you and me.

Menelaus Agreed.

Helen We'll be in heaven.

Menelaus It's really super to see you again.

Helen Now you can take me away.

Menelaus Okay.

Helen But first please tell me you missed me.

Menelaus Oh happy day!

Helen   Together we'll stay.
Menelaus Whatever you say.
Helen   To see you is bliss.
Menelaus Such bliss.
Helen   Just kiss
Menelaus Wow!
Helen   Me quickly!
Menelaus You make me go all prickly inside. Didn't you know?
Helen   Now we can go.
Menelaus Right ho.
Helen   Good show.
Menelaus We'll soon be gone.
Helen   Our boat will float into the rose-coloured dawn.
Menelaus The stars in the sky
Helen   And around every cloud's
Menelaus Oh high
Helen   A silver lining,
Menelaus Spy you and I
Helen   It soon seems right that the moonbeams shine bright,
Menelaus That's true, they're shining
Menelaus⎫ Down from above upon my love. Shine bright, together
Helen   ⎬ On this magic night. For ever with you, we two in heaven.
Chorus   ⎭ A heaven for two.

As the song fades, Agamemnon bursts into tears

Agamemnon That's the most beautiful song I've ever heard. (*He blows his nose, noisily*).
Kid Paris Well, that's real cute of you, Helen.
Priam So now you know, Kid, never trust a woman—or animals!
O'Logarithm Good old horse!
Odysseus Good old Epiglottis.
Agememnon Yes, of course, Private Epiglottis. Fine work, young man. The regiment is proud of you.

The Regiment applaud. Helen and Menelaus, unseen, quietly disappear behind one of the horse's legs

Epiglottis Ta very much.
Agamemnon We must think of a super reward for you. Now, what do you want to be when you grow up? How about a Sergeant-Major?
Achilles Talking of Sergeant-Majors, where's . . .

Suddenly, from the bowels of the earth, there is a distant roar

Platoon Orright! Orright!

Cue 19 *Music—Soppycles' Army Entrance*

A cloud of earth is followed by the entrance of a triumphant Soppycles and his army

Sergeant Major Orright. Hold up yer 'ands. Drop yer money. Shurrup and surrender!

Epiglottis Soppycles!

Tutti Oh, no!

Sergeant-Major Shurrup! Right, you lot. You're surrounded. Get movin' and bring Helen wiv you! Move!

Priam (*to Agamemnon*) Hey. Who's dis guy?

Agememnon Only one of my sergeants. Ignore him.

Sergeant-Major Come on. Where's this Helen?

Helen I'm here.

Sergeant-Major Shurrup!

Helen You mentioned Helen. I'm here.

The Platoon turn and see her. They are stunned to a man

Platoon Gor blimey!

Sergeant-Major Shurrup! (*He turns and sees her. His knees give way*) Gor blimey!

Agamemnon Sergeant-Major, what the devil do you think you're up to?

Sergeant-Major 'Strewth! What the flippin' 'eck are you doin' 'ere, sir? And 'er too?

Agamemnon My dear fellow, it's all over.

Sergeant-Major (*alarmed*) All over what?

Odysseus (*impatiently*) The war's over. That's what.

Achilles So you can get back into your tunnel and go home.

Chef (*sadly*) We're too late, Sarge.

Pythagoras All that diggin' for nothin'.

Sergeant-Major An' we were gonna make 'istory. So much for my knighthood!

Tutti Aaah!

Epiglottis Bad luck, Sarge. It were a good try, though. I've got nothing for you but admiration, Sarge, and very little of that.

Priam Never you mind, Sergeant boy. Come and have a drink with the losers.

Sergeant-Major (*to the world*) There's Southern comfort for you.

Odysseus Let's all have a party!

General approval

What do you say, Menelaus?

Silence. Everyone turns to where Menelaus and Helen had been

Achilles Menelaus, whatever you're doing, stop it at once!

Ajax Quite!

Menelaus appears, slightly dishevelled, from behind one of the horse's legs

Menelaus What's that?

Helen appears and drags him back

(*As he goes*) Oh, golly . . .!

Everyone wolf-whistles

Zippy Zeus leaps on to the stage and up to the microphone

Zippy Zeus Hi there, kids. It's great to be back. Now let's get this party organized. Bring on the booze and let's all start by drinking a toast to Helen.

Tutti Helen!

Zippy Zeus To Menelaus.

Tutti Menelaus!

SONG 20. *FINALE*

Zippy Zeus talks on through the Introduction

Zippy Zeus And to the mightiest horse you ever saw.

Tutti To—the—horse!

During the song, glasses are distributed to the entire company for a final toast to the audience

Greeks What a horse, mightier than any horse you saw before.
What a horse with sauce to end the war with a neigh, say,
Let's ride him home to Greece,
The pride of all who pray for peace.
We can ride him there with this bridal pair. What a horse.

Trojans So this colt ain't no dolt. So you're freed by a steed.
So you get your saddle on, then you paddle on home, so
Many years we've fought the fight and you beat us with a horse
    tonight.
But you know it's true that you owe it all to the horse.

Tutti So while the Trojans all got on the brandy,
Trojan shandy, by the half.
Menelaus for Helen was handy,
What a dandy, what a laugh.
The drunken Trojans couldn't get it together,
They didn't know whether the horse
Was just a joker at a hundred to one
For three o'clock at the Trojan racecourse.

Have a fling, it's the Trojan nag ragtime,
Trojan stag-time has begun.
But just remember that ale turns a Trojan face pale.
With too much boozing, you'll keep on losing,
And while you're snoozing, you'll miss all the fun.

They all toast the audience, as the Lights fade, and—

the Curtain *falls*

A reprise of the final song may be used as a Curtain Call encore

FURNITURE AND PROPERTY LIST

See also Production Notes

PROLOGUE

On stage: Rostra
Small tables with umbrellas. *On them:* various drinks and dishes
Microphone on stand
3 pedestals

Off stage: Tray of drinks (Waiter)

Personal: **Athene:** cigarette in long holder
Zippy Zeus: clipboard

ACT I

On stage: Rostra

Off stage: Bag of jelly-babies (Odysseus)
Spears (Army)
Speech notes (Agamemnon)
Violin case with mini-spear (Ajax)
Speared seagull (Stage Management)
Clipboard (Sergeant-Major)
Swagger stick (Sergeant-Major)
Wrapped toffee (Menelaus)
Bag of toffees (Odysseus)
Plan of "horse" (Epiglottis)
Hammers, chisels, assorted tools (Greek Soldiers)
Bucket, spade (Sergeant-Major)
Baggage (Achilles)
Spear with fish impaled on it—to be placed in violin case (Ajax)
Battle spear (Achilles)
Trick spear (Achilles)
Sections of wooden horse (Soldiers)
Plaster cast (Ajax)
Shovels, picks (Sergeant-Major's Platoon)

ACT II

On stage: Rostra
Trojan Horse (see Production Notes)
Coils of rope
"Twelve Blues Bar", with seats, drinks, glasses, trays (for Waiters)
Ladder concealed by Horse
Microphone

Off stage: Sacks (Greek Soldiers)
Bags of chocolate drops and licorice comfits (Odysseus)
Cloud of earth (Stage Management)

LIGHTING PLOT

See Production Notes
Property fittings required: nil
3 exteriors: a swimming-pool, a seashore, inside the walls of Troy

PROLOGUE Evening

To open: General effect of cool summer evening. Spot-light favour-
ing microphone

No cues

ACT I Early morning

To open: General effect of cold early morning light, becoming warmer
as the Act continues

No cues

ACT II Dawn

To open: Darkness except for backlighting to silhouette Horse

Cue 1   At end of first chorus   (Page 26)
           Snap up full early morning lighting

Cue 2   At end of Finale   (Page 40)
           Fade to Black-out for CURTAIN

NOTE

A suitable "night-club" effect can used for Music Cues 11 and 12. Moonlight
should be used at the end of Music Cues 13 and 14. A follow-spot is useful
for many of the songs

EFFECTS PLOT

PROLOGUE

PRINTED IN GREAT BRITAIN BY
THE LONGDUNN PRESS LTD., BRISTOL.